My Best Book of Gymnastics

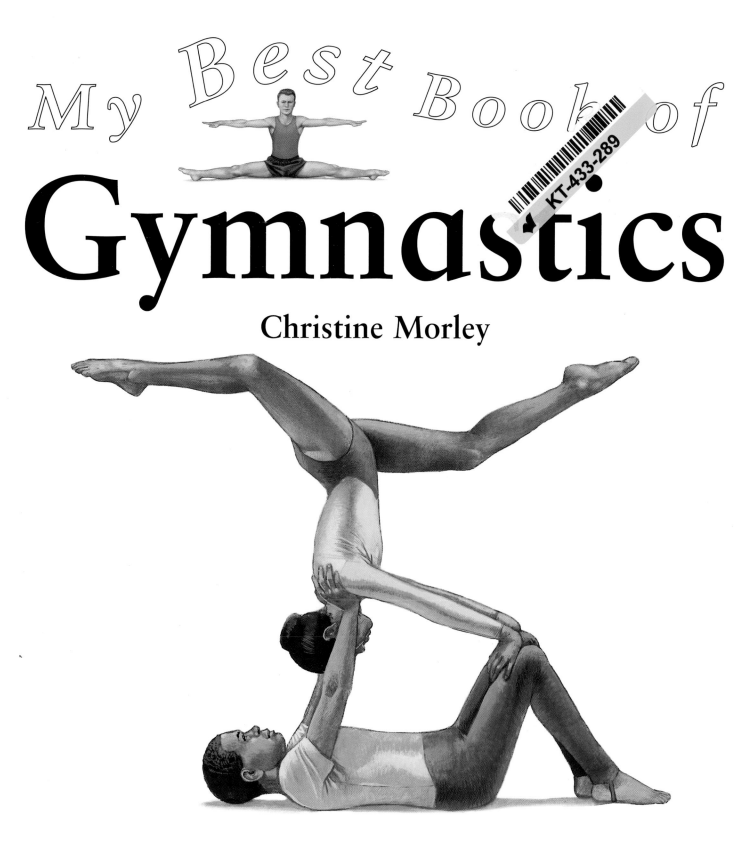

Christine Morley

KINGFISHER

Contents

KINGFISHER

Kingfisher Publications Plc,
New Penderel House,
283–288 High Holborn,
London WC1V 7HZ

www.kingfisherpub.com

Created for Kingfisher by
Picthall & Gunzi Limited

Author: Christine Morley
Designer: Dominic Zwemmer
Editors: Christiane Gunzi and
Lauren Robertson

Illustrator: Michael White,
Consultant: Lloyd Readhead

KINGFISHER
Kingfisher Publications Plc,
New Penderel House,
283–288 High Holborn
London WC1V 7HZ

www.kingfisherpub.com

First published by Kingfisher
Publications Plc 2003

10 9 8 7 6 5 4 3 2 1

1TR/0403/WKT/MAR(MAR)/128/KMA
1TS/0804/WKT/MAR(MAR)/128MA/F

Copyright © Kingfisher
Publications 2003

A CIP catalogue record for this
book is available from the
British Library.

ISBN 0 7534 0835 X

Printed in China

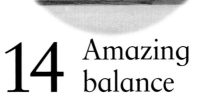

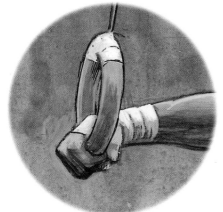
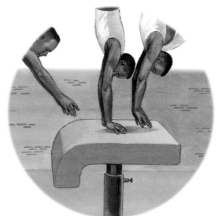

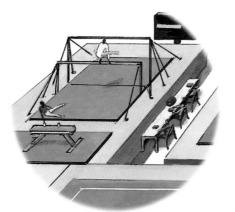

What is gymnastics?

Gymnastics is an enjoyable sport that keeps the body fit. It is done by gymnasts, who perform special movements and shapes that are linked together to make a routine. Gymnastics is divided into disciplines, or styles, including artistic gymnastics, sports acrobatics, trampolining, tumbling and rhythmic gymnastics. Gymnastics is carried out on a floor mat or on apparatus, such as the balance beam and vault. Keen gymnasts can enter competitions.

Pair of sports acrobatic gymnasts performing a balance position

In floorwork, girls and boys train on their own on a padded floor mat.

The pommel horse is used for swings, circles and scissor movements.

The parallel bars are used by male gymnasts only.

Rhythmic gymnastics is set to music and gymnasts use small hand apparatus, such as the ball.

The rings are used in boys' and men's artistic gymnastics.

The horizontal bar is a piece of equipment used only by men.

The asymmetric (uneven) bars are used by women and girls for swings, circles and handstand positions.

The balance beam is used by women. It is only 10cm wide but experienced gymnasts can leap, jump and somersault on it.

The vaulting horse has a non-slip, padded surface that makes it soft and springy.

Death-defying leaps

In Ancient Crete, men and women gymnasts used to leap on to a bull's back, then twist and somersault in mid-air before jumping on to the ground. This was called 'bull leaping'. These movements are like those that gymnasts do on the vault today.

Bull leapers leaping in Ancient Crete, in the second century BCE

The first gymnasts

Gymnastics has been performed since early times. In 3000 BCE, the Ancient Egyptians did vaults and floor exercises, and the Ancient Greeks held tumbling competitions. Soldiers in Ancient China were taught gymnastics as part of their training. When these very old civilizations died out, gymnastics did too. It became popular again in the 1800s.

Medieval acrobatic performers

17th-century acrobatics display

Travelling acrobats

In medieval Europe, gymnastics was practised by travelling performers. They went from town to town, and entertained people with acrobatics, songs, juggling and tricks.

A spectator sport

During the 17th century, entertainers performed acrobatics at the royal courts. They would also perform on stage during the intervals of plays to keep the audience amused.

Getting ready

Many girls and boys learn to do gymnastics at school, where it is taught in physical education.

If you are interested in doing gymnastics, you can join a local gym club, or train for competitions with your school. You can ask about the different kinds of gymnastics and decide which type appeals to you. General gymnastics includes skills from all the different styles. Or you may like to learn a particular kind of gymnastics, such as trampolining.

Finding a coach

Sports clubs often give lessons for beginners. Before choosing a coach or gym club, go along with an adult and watch a class to see if it is right for you.

Instructor and pupils doing a warm-up

Side stretches to work muscles in body and legs

What to wear

As a beginner you can wear shorts and a T-shirt. For competitions, gymnasts wear leotards, which are stretchy and close-fitting, and allow them to move freely. When boys work on the bars or rings, they wear trousers.

Warming up

Training sessions begin with a 10 to 20 minute warm-up to stretch the muscles. It is important to do a warm-up, because if you do not, the muscles and joints could be injured.

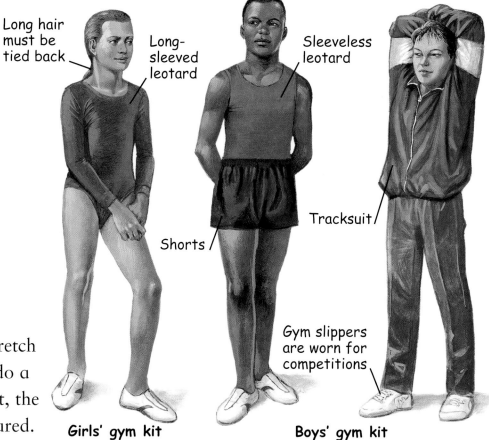

Long hair must be tied back

Long-sleeved leotard

Sleeveless leotard

Shorts

Tracksuit

Gym slippers are worn for competitions

Girls' gym kit

Boys' gym kit

Forward bends to loosen muscles in backs of legs

On the mat

Foam mat for all kinds of floor work

Springboard for extra lift when jumping

Sloping wedge to help move body weight when rolling

Artistic gymnastics is fascinating to watch. The girls work on the vault, asymmetric bars, beam and floor. The boys use the floor, pommel, rings, vault, and parallel bars and horizontal bar. The floor routines include acrobatic and tumbling movements, as well as jumps, leaps and exercises. These moves show flexibility and strength. Traditionally, girls' routines are set to music and include dancing. Boys' exercises include stronger movements and dramatic acrobatics.

Equipment

Floor work takes place on a thick foam mat. It is springy and soft to land on. Sloping wedges of foam are used to help beginners learn rolls. Springboards are for mounting the vault, beam and bars.

Legs are kept in a straight line.

Head points down to the floor.

Feet are pressed firmly into the floor.

The bridge

A gymnast must have strong arms and a flexible back and shoulders to perform this movement. From this position, an experienced gymnast is able to kick her legs over her head to land back on her feet.

Forward roll

Rolling is useful for linking one movement with another. It is best practised on a soft mat. The gymnast starts in a squatting position with the arms stretched forwards and the back straight.

Gymnast leans forwards and puts hands on sides of head to take body weight, tucking in head.

Gymnast gives a push with feet, rolls forwards, then comes back into a squatting position.

Arms and head are off the floor.

Both feet are pointed.

The dish

This develops stomach and leg muscles, and helps to improve posture. The lower back is pressed into the floor. The shoulders, arms and legs are lifted a few centimetres off the ground.

Handstand

To do a handstand well, a gymnast's body must stay straight and still. With enough training, a gymnast is able to perform handstand shapes on the vault, beam, rings and bars.

Handstand on bar

Box splits

In this, the back is straight and the legs are stretched wide to form a straight line. It takes a lot of practice to make the hips and legs supple enough to do this.

Arms can be stretched out wide or above the head.

Box split on floor

Knees turn upwards and toes are pointed.

11

2 After turning a somersault in mid-air, the gymnast straightens out her body to prepare for landing.

Hands are stretched out

1 As the gymnast dismounts from the asymmetric bars, she works up enough speed and power to somersault high in the air.

Body is straight

A difficult dismount means that the judges will give more points.

3 The gymnast holds her arms out wide to control her landing. When she lands, her knees must bend.

Toes are pointed

Jumps and leaps

Gymnasts perform all sorts of breathtaking leaps and jumps on the mat and on apparatus. They are able to make amazing shapes with their bodies in mid-air. Using jumps and leaps, gymnasts link these shapes to impress the judges with their power and style. A jump involves taking off on two feet and landing on two feet. A leap is when the gymnast takes off on one foot but lands on the other foot.

4 As the gymnast lands, she must not wobble or take any extra steps. If she does, she will lose points.

Arms are apart

Knees are bent

Ankles are together

Stag leap

This dramatic shape looks similar to a running stag. It is used in floor and beam work. You can jump from two feet, or take one or two steps forward and then leap.

Straddle pike jump

A gymnast has to jump high in order to have the time to make this difficult shape. It is usually performed on the trampoline and sometimes as a floor exercise.

Amazing balance

To perform balancing positions, such as headstands and handstands, gymnasts need to be strong and able to concentrate very hard. Beginners learn how to balance on the floor with simple exercises, such as raising one leg and holding it still for ten seconds. To learn how to work on the beam, gymnasts train along a line that is drawn on the floor, and then they move on to a low beam. They gradually work on higher levels until they reach a beam 1.25m above the ground.

An 'arabesque' is a balancing position performed on the floor.

1 In an arabesque, the gymnast begins with her arms raised behind the head, making a strong outline with her body.

2 Then the gymnast lifts one leg backwards and points her toes. At the same time, she begins to bring both of her arms forwards.

3 She leans her weight on to the front leg and lifts the free leg up behind her. She lifts her head up and stretches out her arms.

14

On the beam

Balancing on a beam is difficult, and any wobbling is marked down by the judges. Gymnasts must know where to place their feet without looking. This gymnast shows strength, suppleness and balance by making the shape of the letter 'Y' with her body.

The gymnast's supporting leg and foot are very strong.

Beam is only 10cm wide

All kinds of shapes

The shapes that gymnasts make with their bodies must look as attractive as possible. Some shapes, such as the dish, are quite easy to do. Others, such as the bridge, take a lot of practice to perform well. To learn how to do a shape properly, gymnasts sometimes need the help of a 'spotter', who guides and supports them through the movement. To do the back walkover, the gymnast below needs a flexible back and hips.

Toes are pointed

Arms are held out straight

Back walkover on floor

Supporting foot presses into floor

1 The gymnast begins by lifting her right leg out in front of her. She keeps her back straight and arms stretched up above her head.

2 She reaches backwards, and the hips move forwards. During practice, a spotter will support the gymnast as she leans back.

3 Placing her hands on the floor, she points her fingers towards her feet. Her left leg is slightly bent and her right leg points up.

Tight twist

The Yurchenko full twist is named after the gymnast Natalie Yurchenko, who perfected this move. Champions often perform movements with at least one twist.

High handstand

Gymnasts need strength and balance to do a handstand on the parallel bars and rings. They must hold the position for at least two seconds. This male gymnast is practising on parallettes.

Leg is brought down smoothly

A split-legs handstand

Gymnast keeps an extended body shape

4 The gymnast takes her weight on to her hands as she pushes up with her left leg. She brings her right leg down towards the floor.

5 As the gymnast's right leg reaches the floor, her left leg keeps moving back. Her toes must be kept pointed at all times.

6 When both of her feet are back on the ground, the gymnast stands tall, raises her arms, points her hands back and smiles!

17

The cross

Only male gymnasts use the rings. Their ring routines must include swinging exercises with at least two handstands. This advanced position is called the cross. A beginner can practise this if a helper holds his ankles and supports his weight.

Legs are held in straight line and kept close together

High in the air

The most dramatic movements are performed high in the air on the rings and the bars.

Female gymnasts use the asymmetric bars, and male gymnasts work on the parallel bars and the horizontal bar. They make moves such as somersaults, swings and twists. They also do release and catch moves. Gymnasts' dismounts are always spectacular to watch.

Handstand balance

Handstand balance

The handstand balance is a difficult position that takes a huge amount of strength. To perform it correctly, the gymnast must keep his ankles, knees, hips and shoulders in a straight line.

Protecting the hands

Gymnasts often wear handguards to stop their hands becoming sore. The handguards fit over the fingers and fasten around the wrists. Gymnasts also use chalk to soak up sweat on their hands and feet, so that they do not slip.

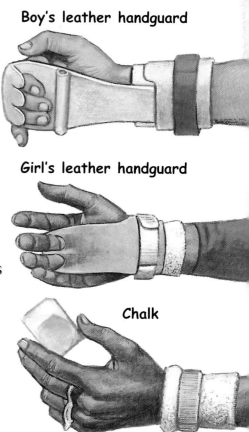

Boy's leather handguard

Girl's leather handguard

Chalk

On the horses

In gymnastics, 'horses' are pieces of apparatus that gymnasts leap over. Long ago, they were shaped like real horses, with a head and neck, but they do not look like that today. In competitions, gymnasts use the vaulting horse, or vaulting table, which is a padded platform. The pommel is another type of horse. The horses are all quite soft and springy.

Body stays straight as gymnast flies forward

Body is straight as gymnast springs upwards

Gymnast jumps up high from springboard

Hands are placed on horse for handstand

Handspring vault

The handspring vault is an advanced move for boys and girls. With enough height and speed, experienced gymnasts can leap through the air, land on their hands on the vault, then spring off and land upright on their feet again.

The pommel horse

The pommel horse stands 115cm high.
It is very difficult to use and needs
great concentration and strength.
The gymnast must swing his body
across and around the horse,
balancing on one hand. His legs
must never touch the pommel horse.

Male gymnast using pommel horse

Legs are kept
together with
toes pointed

**Other gymnasts waiting
for their turn to perform**

Knees
are bent

Body and
legs are
straight

21

Music and dance

One of the most graceful forms of gymnastics is rhythmic gymnastics, performed by girls and women.

Dance or ballet-style moves are carried out to music, while the gymnasts use pieces of hand equipment, such as ribbons and hoops. Rhythmic gymnasts work with the music and bring their own style to the routine.

Using ribbons and hoops

Rhythmic gymnasts work on their own or in groups of up to six people. Girls in the group can use different hand apparatus, which they pass, throw and roll to each other. In a group competition, the gymnasts have between two-and-a-half and three minutes to complete the routine.

The gymnast can make beautiful shapes with the ribbon, but it must not touch her body or become tangled.

Types of hand apparatus

The five pieces of hand apparatus are balls, ropes, clubs, ribbons and hoops. The ribbon is probably the most popular apparatus, and the clubs are the most difficult and dangerous to use. Whichever items the gymnast uses, she must keep them moving at all times.

Ball for balancing on the hands, feet or body

Rope for skipping and jumping

Clubs for juggling and throwing

Hoop is made of plastic or wood

Ribbon is made of satin and is about 7m long

The gymnast moves the hoop over and around her body, rolls it, throws it in the air and catches it.

Trampoline training

Gymnasts spend hours on the trampoline practising their routines. They use the same basic movements and somersaults as those in artistic gymnastics. A coach corrects any mistakes.

Coach giving instructions

Gymnast stays as high as she can when performing moves

Skilful somersaults

 **In trampolining, gymnasts do daring movements, such as very high somersaults.** In Sydney, Australia, in 2000, this became an Olympic sport. Tumbling is an older sport and is also exciting to watch. Gymnasts run on a track to build up power, and then do a series of somersaults and twists in only six seconds. It takes years of hard work for a gymnast to perform for just a few, thrilling seconds.

Terrific tumblers

In 1932, tumbling was an Olympic sport. It is no longer an Olympic sport, but gymnasts can enter championships. In competitions, they perform three runs, showing twists, somersaults and a combination of both. The best tumblers can do three double somersaults plus twists in a single run!

Working as a team

Sports acrobatics is a type of gymnastics that developed from acrobatic circus displays. It involves balance and tumbling skills. Girls and boys do routines on a floor mat in pairs, or in threes and fours. There are balance exercises to do, and also exercises called tempo. Tempo is where one gymnast performs somersaults, twists and turns while being thrown into the air by her partner.

Triple balance

Girls perform balances in pairs or in groups of three. Here, they are doing a dramatic triple balance.

The judges give marks for strength, steadiness and style. In competitions, each balance must be held for at least two seconds.

The legs can be straight or bent.

The back and arms must be straight.

'Top' rests hands on knees of 'base' to keep arms steady

'Base' has back and feet in stable position

Working in pairs

When gymnasts work together in pairs, the person who is supporting the weight is called the 'base', and the person who is being supported is called the 'top'. This pair of gymnasts is performing the shoulder balance.

26

The mid-position person balances on his arms, and his legs are free.

The top balances on one arm with the weight of his body resting on one elbow.

Four-man pyramid

Adult male gymnasts perform in twos, threes or fours. Here, a team of four is doing a spectacular pyramid in front of a panel of judges. Advanced balancing routines like this are accompanied by music and last for up to two and a half minutes.

WARNING!
You cannot teach yourself gymnastics. Do not try to do these advanced moves until you have attended classes.

The bases stand with their legs firmly on the ground and their arms stretched out for balance.

Watching displays

There are many opportunities to see gymnastic displays. You can watch competitions between schools and clubs, or go to events such as championships. Major events, including the Olympics, are shown on television. You can also watch gymnastics at the circus. The famous Chinese State Circus tours the world with its daring teams of acrobats and balance artists.

Champion acrobats

Acrobatic displays have been practised in China for more than 2,000 years. The Chinese State Circus acrobats use objects, such as chairs and hoops, to perform incredible feats of strength and balance. These are really exciting to watch.

Acrobats forming a human pyramid

Cheerleaders performing balancing act

Ra-ra-ra!

Cheerleaders entertain crowds at football matches in the USA. They chant rhymes to their team while they do leaps, splits and balances with props such as batons.

Acrobat doing high back flip through hoop

Acrobat balancing on a pole, using only one hand

Gymnastics events

Modern gymnastics competitions have been held for more than a hundred years. The biggest events are the Olympic Games and World Championships. There are also competitions between clubs and schools, with events for all ages and levels. Even if you are not competing, gymnastics events are great fun to watch and you can pick up tips from the experts!

Competition layout

All the events are on a stage 90cm high. The apparatus is laid out so that officials can see the gymnasts clearly. Judges award points based on how difficult a move is and how well it is done.

Scoreboard

Asymmetric bars

Balance beam

Pommel horse

Area around stage for practising and warming up

Floor mat

Vaulting horse

Rings

Horizontal bar

Parallel bars

Judges' area at sides of stage

Glossary

apparatus The different types of equipment used in gymnastics, such as the beam or bars. Hand apparatus is used in rhythmic gymnastics.

asymmetric bars A piece of apparatus used by girls. It has two bars at different heights.

balancing Holding the body still, without falling over.

base In sports acrobatics, the name for the gymnast who supports the weight of another.

beam A narrow bar on which gymnasts perform different moves and balances.

chalk A fine white powder that gymnasts dust on their hands and feet to help them grip.

disciplines The different types of gymnastics that have developed over the years. These types include artistic gymnastics, rhythmic gymnastics, tumbling, trampolining, sports acrobatics and sports aerobics.

dismount The last move in a routine, when the gymnast jumps off a beam or bar.

flexible Being able to bend the body easily.

handguards Soft leather protectors worn on the hands.

horse The padded apparatus that gymnasts vault over.

mount To get on to a piece of apparatus.

parallettes Pieces of equipment used for practising handstands.

pike A V-shaped position made by bending the body at the hips.

posture The way that a person holds their body.

rhythmic gymnastics A type of gymnastics with a floor routine set to music, and hand apparatus, such as a ribbon or ball.

routine A set of moves that are joined together.

somersault A full turn of the body that is performed in mid-air.

spotter A trained person who helps a gymnast to practise their positions.

squat A position where a person crouches with the knees bent and with the bodyweight on the feet.

straddle A position where the legs are stretched out wide apart.

tempo A type of exercise that is performed in sports acrobatics.

top In sports acrobatics, the top is the gymnast who is balancing on another gymnast.

tumbling A discipline that involves somersaults and twists.

warm-up Gentle exercises that prepare the body for exercise.

Index

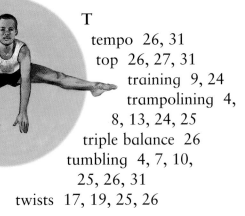

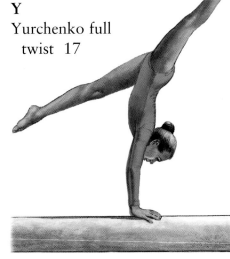